THE QUARANTINE KATHAS - THE BLOGGER'S VERSION

BASED ON THE EXPERIENCE OF
ASHMITHA ARUNKUMAR

ANUMANTHRAM S

Copyright © Anumanthram S
All Rights Reserved.

ISBN 978-1-63873-055-2

This book has been published with all efforts taken to make the material error-free after the consent of the author. However, the author and the publisher do not assume and hereby disclaim any liability to any party for any loss, damage, or disruption caused by errors or omissions, whether such errors or omissions result from negligence, accident, or any other cause.

While every effort has been made to avoid any mistake or omission, this publication is being sold on the condition and understanding that neither the author nor the publishers or printers would be liable in any manner to any person by reason of any mistake or omission in this publication or for any action taken or omitted to be taken or advice rendered or accepted on the basis of this work. For any defect in printing or binding the publishers will be liable only to replace the defective copy by another copy of this work then available.

Dedicated to all those who have given their lives for humanity.

Dedicated to all the frontline workers of COVID-19

Dedicated to social media and its followers

Contents

Acknowledgements vii

Prologue ix

1. The First Impression   1
2. I Wasn't Ready Da!   11
3. Him   16
4. They Love Me 3000   20
5. Wo(aḥ)men   31
6. Bundles To Betterment   43

Acknowledgements

The first one to thank would be God, for everything that he has given me.

All the people I thank below were my strength while I was writing this book and play a prominent role in my life.

My parents for the everlasting support, they have given me. For standing with every insane thing I came up in my life.

My friends like family at Mumbai, Bangalore and Dharmapuri for all the help, the companionship that they gave throughout my journey.

To Department of Biotechnology, PSG College of Technology, for bearing all my menaces in my UG followed by other faculty of PSG College of Technology, my fellow batchmates, seniors and classmates for sculpting me through years.

To the lockdown and the novel coronavirus 19 for spoiling my plans and giving me the time to think and come up with this series.

To all those who worked in this pandemic to raise the wall against the virus and to those who have laid down their lives in the fight against the virus.

To the sweetest blogger – Ashmitha Arunkumar for accepting my request and sparing her time in editing and reviewing the book.

To Instagram and all its followers for providing a platform for millions to connect and share their skills.

To all the readers of my debut book – The Incomplete Diary, for their support and feedback.

Prologue

It was time. Time to rest, to relax and to enjoy life. The initial two months of the year 2020 kept me busy, preparing for the ACCA exams and finally, I was done with it. I returned to India from the US in the wake of 2020 and began preparing for my ACCA exams. I went through similar pressure back in June 2019 during my university exams in Singapore. It wasn't easy playing the academic role.

Regardless of the time, we get in advance, the last-minute preparations are the ones that save. I was no exception; I was someone who prepared better driven by fear than by any other means. After hectic exams from the University, binge shopping in the US, I got to India in January and ACCA exams were around the corner.

It wasn't something sudden and I knew the tentative schedule of the exams. For some reason, my mind wanted the stress, the tension to prepare. It wouldn't get exam ready otherwise. So from January, I sat for days and nights alike to cover the portions of the exam.

Becoming an accountant was more difficult than being one, it needed a lot of efforts. I sat days and nights alike to prepare for ACCA with the fear of failure being the ultimate driving force. I sacrificed social media, television and everything apart from studying. It was more of a penance than preparation.

I could have eased the load and the stress by preparing long back but my mind wasn't ready to do it. I did my penance for the next 2 months and in the mid of March, I was relieved of ACCA. It was time to rest, party and chill. I was trying to shift from the exam me to the leisure me. It

PROLOGUE

indeed was a true bliss – to do nothing at home, ease on the couch watch movies, television series, browse through the net and laze off. It was more of the retired life that I was living after my exams. It was around that time when I knew about the pandemic going haywire in the USA, China and Italy. I was amused at the tissue paper hoarding in the USA, the lack of beds in hospitals in Italy. I left it to my wildest imagination, the chaos the virus would cause in a country like India.

Things that follow after this are the reactions and the responses in the whelm of the pandemic Covid 19

CHAPTER I

The First Impression

After the spread of the outbreak in China, the US and Italy, the rest of the world got serious. Cases were growing every hour and this rise was geometric instead of arithmetic. I wasn't able to keep a check on the news due to my exams but after exams, this happened to be one of my biggest roles. I followed the news closely to know about the spread of the pandemic around the world. I knew that India wasn't far behind and keeping the population density of India in mind, the virus could cause immense chaos. In a week after, the news featured cases of covid-19 in the major cities of the country like Delhi and Mumbai.

It was time for superstition and rumours to take over. In India, we make our reasons and give our own explanation to any worldwide incident, we criticize science and give out superstition. Sadly, once a few times it turns co-incidental and the people of the country are more to believe such superstitions and stupid logics than to settle for scientific facts. One such rumour was that the novel coronavirus is ineffective in high temperature and would die in India because of the soaring temperatures of summer.

To their dismay, cases were first reported in Rajasthan (the hottest state of the country). Many such beliefs and false facts circulated through social media and there were some rituals done in temples to kill a virus. Such facts grabbed the attention of media and the press and the people enjoyed doing weird things to get rid of the virus. I tried to explain the facts, soon lost my cool and left it to their own brains to figure out the facts.

Coimbatore wasn't far with the fact that the virus had travelled all the way from China in a matter of weeks. It was at that time when the Prime Minister of India announced a 21-day lockdown to control and prevent the spread of the coronavirus in the subcontinent. Instagram and Facebook were more active in taking the news to the people faster than the news channels or newspapers. In seconds after the announcement of the lockdown, there were memes on Instagram about the lockdown. I liked and shared a few among my friends and family. Though there was fear attached to the virus, we didn't want to waste time, so we decided to call for a family reunion. I didn't get the time to meet all my relatives after I landed in India because of my exams and saw this as an opportunity to meet and interact with them. That was our first response to lockdown.

Meeting my relatives in a single spot instead of visiting them individually was fun raised to an exponential level. The men in the house were busy with serious discussions about news and politics while the women were busy decorating the table with yummy, delicious dishes. In the meantime, I was busy explaining my experiences in Singapore, US – about the exams, education and lifestyle to my cousins. This was amongst the perk of being the oldest kid in the family, everyone looks upon to you as their inspiration and guiding light. Time spent with family is indeed the best time that one could get. With my cousins and relatives around, it was really difficult to keep track of time.

We had a lot of fun together as a family. Social media kept us entertaining with all the memes on lockdown and the effects of lockdown. Some memes criticized the government for announcing the lockdown and for bringing down the economy of the country, while there were a few tweets by doctors and researchers who advocated on the necessity of lockdown in a populous country like India and somewhere confused between these two extremes the citizens of the country were dealing with the pandemic.

There wasn't anything that we could do in particular in the lockdown. I was only an accountant in the making and the government wasn't really in need of us. The only thing we could do was to stay put in our homes and we were doing that as a family with fun and frolic. The impact that the lockdown had on us was also very less as we were all inside our homes and there weren't any external stimuli involved. These were among the perks of living in a gated community, we had very less interaction with the city as the roads in our community weren't public and attracted very less traffic. As the cases in the country slowly began increasing, fear spread around the city and soon reached us. We had to stay isolated from the other parts of the city to ensure safety and most of that was guaranteed by our community protocols.

The only interaction our community members had was via the house help who came from the slums near our community. We decided to stop the maids from getting into our homes to make sure that we were double safe and secure. The provisions came via the security to our houses and that was safer than risking exposure in the stores. We came together as an extended family and ordered all our provisions in bulk consulting all the houses in our community to reduce the risk to the front liners. No house help meant that we had to do our chores in the house which posed a more serious threat, as it meant everyone in the house had to share our roles in cooking, cleaning and washing. It was difficult to manage the house. It was during this time that I realized the role that our mothers play in our house. Mom couldn't do all house chores by herself so we had to volunteer, I agreed to clean my room while my dad was helping mom with the sweeping and mopping.

Dad was doing the house chores for the first time, as there always was house help to carry these roles and though dad kept complaining, he had very little of a choice. We weren't pleased in doing our roles but we cant simply shoulder off all our responsibility. The lockdown went day after the other and we were getting desperate to come out. We checked onto news channels once a while to know about the areas affected and about the spread of the virus. The spread in Mumbai, Delhi was astonishing as the cases reached from 100s to 1000s in few days while a few cases popped up daily in Coimbatore. Coimbatore is a city close to Kerala and among the most prominent cities of the state. The fact that the first case in our country surfaced at Kerala added to our worry. If the virus was to visit Tamilnadu from Kerala then Coimbatore can't be missed. This still increased the risk for the residents.

We were bored and out of hobbies. Then Modiji announced tasks that could be done from our houses and ready we were, to carry out the tasks like participants of the reality show Big Boss. The first task was to clap hands from our houses for the frontline workers who were working day and night to control this pandemic. We assembled in the balcony and clapped our hands and waved the torch in our mobiles to the sky expressing our gratitude. In the news, we could see people going a step ahead and banging plates and cutlery and a few resorted to jamming the horns in the vehicles especially in the northern part of the country. The following week, a new task was assigned by the political head of our country. It was to light lamps in and around our homes. Thanks to Indian spammers and astrologers, there were a zillion rumours that were spread on WhatsApp groups and social media on these lamps.

The funniest one I heard was a forward message that stated that the lights from the lamps emit radiation that would kill the virus and prevent the spread, hence the prime minister had asked us to light it. Though the literate part of me found lighting lamps only as a source of hope and motivation to those who were in the frontlines and to those who were affected, I found it these myths and beliefs interesting. This was the last of activities offered by the Prime minister. I believe he must have seen one such mythical forward message and that must have made him stop these weekly tasks. That was the power superstition had in India.

Boredom came back in, the major television networks in India stopped broadcasting new episodes due to restrictions in shooting, now even the elderly population found it difficult to adapt to the lockdown and got restless. It was at a time of ultimate boredom, joblessness and longing to travel when I switched to OTT series. It was complete entertainment in a nutshell. There were hundreds of series, different seasons to a single series and had an end. This was going to save me from lockdown. I got on my bed with my laptop, installed all the applications necessary and logged in. I began watching one series after the other to kill time, my favourite series was Brooklyn 99 and New girl. If it wasn't for this lockdown then I never would have got the time to watch them. From watching series to kill time, I slowly began killing time to watch series, that was how these series got me and I began dedicating my entire day to such series. I can't advocate or recommend on watching series stating a few are educative, have unique content, knowledgeable but if you are someone who has enough time to kill then you can always resort to series. They help remove boredom.

One another item on the trend list this lockdown was the game - ludo. The ludo king app in the play store saw a huge rise in the downloads and was among the highest downloaded games on play store for a short period. There was nothing new in this game like the adventure games and it didn't have mind-blowing graphics or media like PUBG or wasn't an extended-release of some super-duper PC game like Call Of Duty, but it was just a digitalized version of a very old game that we and our past generations would have grown up with. It was just another board game similar to chess just that it wasn't as complex as chess.

I remember playing ludo as a child, on a board with 4 different coloured squares and paths to the middle of the board. It was going viral around the country and maybe around the whole world because the rules of the game were known to all, the app was light in terms of space, interactive and could be played online among friends. So apart from TV series, this was my other medicine to combat lockdown. This game not only helped me kill time but also helped me to stay in touch with my buddies in Singapore. I played ludo king almost every evening with my friends from Singapore and was soon excelling it. Though the game is based on luck, my friends accused me of cheating as I always got the number 6 on my dice which was the trump number to unlock a coin and has an extra roll of dice.

There was also virtual betting with game coins. Though these coins had no value out of the game, it was a matter of life or death to win the game. It was more of pride than sport. Not just the youth but even the elders in the house found it difficult to resist the game and began playing it with their friends and relatives who were held in other parts of the world. For them, it was the nostalgia of their childhood. The initial versions of the game had very few options and could only be played amongst people passing the device without network usage but soon the updates made it possible to connect among friends by sharing a particular code for the corresponding room.

This wasn't the only game to gain popularity in the lockdown. The craze for PUBG and COD remained among the 2k kids, the multiplayer and battle royale modes in Call Of Duty addressed the boredom of the modern generation. They were crazier and more involved in locating and collecting airdrops than they would have ever prepared for their academics. The major disadvantage of these military-based action games was that they were very heavy on memory and battery, irrespective of the specification phones found it difficult to conserve battery as they had high graphics and visual effects.

Though there was lockdown imposed in the country, there was no halt to the number of cases of the novel coronavirus. There was also no end to those infringed the lockdown, the news showed people who came out of their houses, for the fun of roaming out. They weren't serious about the pandemic and considered themselves stronger than the virus. The cops clamped down such outlaws and gave them funny punishments like rolling on the road, squatting for a long time, kneeling and a lot more.

One other thing that I witnessed in this lockdown, was the dedicated service of the frontline workers to society. It must be someone, someone has to get into the field, someone has to work, everything cant be carried out via work from home and these people had to do it. It was their duty to do and they were doing it as better as possible. To start with the doctors, they were no superhumans. They just have an MBBS degree behind their names and for the sake of humanity, they had to work during the times such as the pandemic. I could relate to the hardships faced by doctors because most of my relatives from the paternal side are doctors including my paternal grandparents. Doctors have to deal with covid positive patients and the risks of getting infected are much higher than others but it was their profession and this could be termed as an occupational hazard. A few doctors were working for hours together, without proper rest and break to get the virus under control and to save the lives of patients.

When working in this havoc itself is threatening, in a tropic country like India roaming around the hospital premises in PPE kit doubles the difficulty. It isn't easy covering one's entire body with plastic and performing daily activities but it was necessary as this was among the few means by which they can reduce the risk of infection. As I scrolled through the stories and news feed, I saw pictures of doctors face turning pale after wearing those kits for hours together and there were impression lines of the mask on their face.

PPE kits weren't new, as most of the major surgeries require a sterile environment and to ensure that doctors had to wear PPE but operation theatres are air-conditioned removing temperature and humidity from the equation. Our country burns in the summer and the virus can spread faster through the conditioner. Hence doctors have to bear the heat and their duty time at the minimum is 6-8 hours, so they have to be in the kit for that time. It also isn't possible to attend nature calls normally as this wraps up the person from tip to toe. They have to use adult diapers and using them isn't as easy as we think. Amongst all such issues, they must offer their help to their patients and carry out their roles.

The next important frontline workers are the cops. Times like this are a golden opportunity for crime to happen and to maintain the decorum of the city, these men and women must perform their duty, come what may. No matter how worse they get trolled for accepting bribes, favouring the rich, following orders blindly, they did their best in discharging their duties this lockdown and did the maximum possible to keep the order of the city. The worst part they had to do was to deal with the public who went out often, infringing the lockdown rules. While these cops had no choice than to come out for their duty, people disobeying rules and roaming around in the roads instead of staying at the comfort of their homes was disheartening.

There are a lot of other professionals who acted in this lockdown but these three were the most important. They knew the risks of the disease, they knew the chances of getting infected were high, they knew that the novel coronavirus could get fatal, but still, they chose to discharge their duties.

I heard about a few from the frontlines, not being able to return to their homes as they could act as a carrier of this virus. They might have a strong immune power that could withstand and put up a fight against the virus but not everyone in their homes could have the same. There might be newborn children who would have no immunity and the virus can infect them, there could be old people parents or grandparents who would have lost their immune strength with age and there also could be immune-compromised individuals like those suffering from arthritis, organ transplantation and more. The virus could take a toll on them, it was the duty of these frontline workers to discharge duty but that doesn't mean that their families had to take the risk and hence many chose to stay out of their homes, stay isolated. News, memes, audio, video of such people not just inspired me but raised the respect that I had on them.

CHAPTER II
I wasn't ready da!

When the lockdown 1.0 was nearing an end in April, we wanted to go out, execute the plans we made in our calendar, live the life and pursue our dreams. It was summer and time for a vacation. There was a large to-do list on my mind but our government had other ideas. They extended the lockdown with a few relaxations. It was lockdown 2.0. When we weren't ready to take 21 days of lockdown, this second lockdown brought down all our hopes of vacation. It was for the greater good, as the virus was still on the loose and hundreds were getting affected by it every single day, so we had to confine ourselves inside for another 21 days.

The government was announced a few relaxations to the lockdown, to facilitate our lives and meet our daily needs if not for luxury. One person in the family was allowed to go out for grocery and provisions. The curfew was eased in the morning for this purpose, we must get back to our homes before noon and shops would be closed after that time. There were a lot of such restrictions announced in the opening and closing of shops and markets. The central grocery markets in the city were shut down fearing the spread of the virus. The market was divided and small mini markets shops were set up every 2 km radius, to facilitate people of that area to shop groceries. There were also mobile vegetable trucks that went around the streets to deliver groceries.

One person from our family had to step out to get the essentials and I was the first one to be ruled out because

I wasn't the early morning type and was the apple of my parent's eye. Mom took up the role. We believed in getting vegetables fresh daily in the morning owing to the health benefits but when getting vegetables itself was a luxury one cant demand fresh stuff, so we stocked up vegetables and provisions for a week at least. Mom went out in the morning once a week, for provisions and groceries and immediately took a shower on return. This was our schedule for the next 3 weeks and our mom was our saviour.

She was undoubtedly the healthiest person in our family. When I found it really difficult to get ready and move on with my daily roles, she took care of the entire family and also spent time for her health. She's a very active woman and played badminton almost every day which made her eligible to travel out for essentials. She wasn't the giving up type and that ended up to be both a boon and a bane for me.

She expected a part of her fitness in me, which was a very big deal. I was more of the 2k kid's type or in her words the couch potato kind. I really loved to laze around and wasn't the fitness lover. When mom and daughter stay together the whole day with nothing great to do, have different ideas on health then the obvious outcome would be quarrels and that was something more common in this lockdown. The most important trigger for these quarrels would be on fitness and not being active enough.

Such quarrels with mom never had an end, because they are our mothers and anything that they tell or do would be for our good, in the meantime transition from a couch potato to a fitness freak can't happen in a month. I have been this couch potato for a long time that it more turned to my lifestyle so I had to argue to defend though I knew she was right. She was concerned about my health. Every single issue that I ever raised at home was directly connected to my fitness and that made me feel as if my head was being eaten. These quarrels make me miss home and mom. Memories aren't just sweet and cheesy moments but quarrels, compromises and consolation too. I little did know while arguing that I would miss that irritation very soon.

Tamilnadu was booming with cases next to Maharashtra and the cases in the capital city were massive. 1000-2000 cases were booming every single day. Though lockdown was in effect, the people in Chennai, gladly neglected the lockdown rules hoping it to be another hoax by the government. By the time the residents understood the heat of the situation, there were more than 40% listed and much more in loose. The government then had to adopt stricter measures by closing and relocating major markets, bazaars and other necessities.

We were worried about our relatives in Chennai seeing the news of hundreds turning positive. We reached them on call to make sure they were safe and that was all that we could do against a virus. We can't get to Chennai or bring them here with this lockdown in effect so all we could do was to pray for their betterment and safety. Not all wishes get granted, a few of my relatives turned positive for corona and were taken to the nearest hospitals. We tried our best to boost their morale and, in a few weeks,, they got back on their toes. They were discharged from hospitals and placed under home quarantine.

The relaxation in the lockdown was to facilitate the residents to get all that they need and it didn't mean the virus was gone. The virus was still there, amongst the crowd, amongst the people, amongst everything and everywhere but people took these relaxations as a relaxation in the spread of the virus. A few of our neighbours began re-employing maids or house help into their homes. It might have not been easy for the residents to manage all domestic work but that was no reason for allowing others into the community at a crisis like this.

This not only poses a threat to their own family but might risk a chance of infection for other families in the area too. There are senior citizens and newborns in our community and they are more prone to the virus. These maids generally came from a nearby slum where a great question of sanitation and hygiene arises. The people in the slums are unlikely to contradict covid19 because of their strong immune power acquired by dealing with a wide range of microbes in their day to day environment and their living conditions. This doesn't mean they can't carry the virus, they might act as carriers of the virus and spread it amongst the people.

I expected 2020 to be different, way too different. There were a lot of things that I had in my mind for the year. Aakash and I were to get married in June, I had plans to go to the US, Aakash had plans for flight training, I wanted to take a few steps in my discipline, to clear a few more ACCA levels but this year turned it all down. The start of this year began with bush fire, then a possible threat of a world war, death of a famous basketball player, accidents and then pandemic that took over for the rest of the year. Not just me, but everyone would have had plans for this year and I'm pretty sure that this year was beyond their wildest expectations.

I expected my cousins to return from the USA at the end of May, we had planned on spending time together, having fun but all in vain. They couldn't get to India because of the pandemic. The wedding we expected was much different from the one that we had and Aakash had to skip his flight training which was expected to happen that year. I could have cleared two more ACCA levels if not for the pandemic, at least by turning to a vampire preparing day and night for the exam.

There is still hope, good in every bad. My schedule for 2020 wasn't something that can't be done in the coming years and so I decided to reschedule, postpone my plans for the year. It would have been good if things went as per the plan but it's better when life gives us surprises and I am looking forward to a few. I have postponed my ACCA exams to 2021 provided the situation gets back to normal or we get used to the new normal. I have decided to postpone the US trip sometime near summer, once I sort out my academics in the UK.

CHAPTER III

Him

I can never decide on what to tell or what not to tell when it comes to Aakash. I asked him out on June 4, 2015, and then began our love story. We have been together for five years and that is a lot of time when compared to relationships these days. They meet each other in the morning, propose over breakfast, date till lunch, break up in the night and move on. Our love wasn't made in china type and lasted long. We aren't perfect but we are made for each other, he has always supported me be it Singapore, India or anywhere in the world.

Staying together in a relationship isn't easy unless there is trust and love. There exist a Romeo to every Juliet, a Dante to every Beatrice and an Anthony to every Cleopatra, it just takes time and luck to discover the right person and for me it was Aakash. He has been with me throughout my journey and knew me better than anyone in this world and vice versa. From sharing the skincare products that I get to sharing our lives we have come a long way and have an even longer way to go.

I could see people posting on social media about the effect of lockdown on their relationships. The ones close to their loved ones made them pregnant while the ones away from each other developed issues and a few issues got so serious that it went till break up. There were very few amongst the ones I knew to have a strong long-distance relationship. We had our base strong and secured with love and trust. This pandemic wasn't the only time we were separated, we have been in a long-distance relationship since long and I knew of the problems better than others. We did have issues between us, we fought fiercely, went through heartbreaks which made us hate each other, but we always had the big picture in our mind. That kept our relationship going amongst all odds. We had our regular text sessions, calls and video calls, so we were fine in this pandemic.

Amongst the issues, our relationship faced in this lockdown, the most important one was the quarantine period. Aakash landed in India post lockdown and as per the guidelines he was placed under quarantine for 14 days. I would state that to be the most stressful and depressing part of the lockdown, to see him confined in a room for 14 days. He was confined in a hotel room for 14 whole days. Though the room was super good, when placed in confinement no luxury can match freedom. I did my part to keep him motivated by calling via voice and video, texting and doing all that was possible to remove his loneliness. The further worst part of the institutional isolation was the diet. He had to have 14 days of vegetarian and that was something really difficult for him. He wanted me on call 24*7 and I did my best to be there for him. It is these small things in a relationship that make it sweet.

After two weeks of quarantine and a strict vegetarian diet, my better half was back to me. We met 4 days before our wedding and I could finally sense the wedding vibes around. My wedding – corona didn't let that too in peace. We were in the third phase of lockdown when my wedding came. There were mixed opinions of postponing the wedding, shifting it to next year and so on but we didn't want to miss the moment. This was something I was looking forward to 5 years and I didn't want to lose or postpone the moment. My dream wedding from my childhood wasn't on a cruise, or a palace or at a star hotel, I wanted my wedding to happen at my ancestral house in Tirunelveli with my close friends and family around. I wasn't interested in the big fat Indian wedding type. The wedding we planned pre-lockdown was different and more of the grand type, though I wasn't inclined to spend a fortune on it.

The pandemic spoilt it all and we had to call only our close relatives, friends and people around Coimbatore. We couldn't have proper wedding shopping, as we weren't allowed to roam around the city and that was the first setback our wedding took. We went with all that we could arrange. The worst part was Aakash's parents weren't able to attend the wedding. They were stuck in Qatar and there weren't any flights available for them to travel to India, so the wedding had to go on without them. This was another setback. Aakash's uncle (his father's brother) and aunt managed to make it to our wedding on behalf of my in-laws. Aakash's parents were amongst the priorities in our family and they were much missed that day.

Another setback was that my paternal relatives weren't able to make it to my wedding. This was another lacuna in the marriage chapter of my life. There were lot others in that space and they tried to fill that gap but things don't work that way, people can't be replaced. My close friends from Tirupur somehow made it to the wedding. We knew each other from school so no matter what they would make it to my wedding. They were the fun factor in the wedding and kept the joy on.

My wedding turned from big fat to budget, thanks to the pandemic and to Chinese brothers and sisters for giving the world this virus. The unpredictable turn of events somehow matched my expectation of a compact wedding.

The wedding went on without a few VIPs and thanks to the technology they were at least able to watch it via video call. That was one another innovation that we had at our wedding generally, there exists video coverage of the wedding but our wedding had video call coverage for my paternal relatives and his parents. That was something that we could do. These people would never have missed our wedding because they were that close to us but this pandemic did this, giving me one another reason to hate the virus.

Another part of my wedding was that it happened to come a day after my birthday, saving the expense to host a party. This was getting more and more budget-friendly. The emotion remained the same between me and Aakash though the venue and the celebrations changed. There were a few relatives who managed to make it to the wedding as they were residing close by. My parents did everything possible to make the wedding as good as possible and amongst all setbacks, we were pronounced as husband and wife with the blessings of the almighty. On the last week of June began our official journey as a couple. It wasn't a dream wedding but a wedding among dreams.

Above everyone, I had Aakash and he had me. That was the whole thing about the relationship and for the tradition, we had everything in place so our marriage was technically done. He was the most supportive person one could ask for and wish for in life. Even if the whole world was against me, I was sure that this guy would stand beside me and I would do the same for him. The journey was going to be no different from before, as we already had the understanding and love in us.

CHAPTER IV

They love me 3000

Self-love is the highest form of love one can possess. Only when one can love the person he or she is, they would be able to love others.

Self-love aids a person to become better physically and psychologically, making him/her more presentable. When you love yourself, the way you look at the mirror changes, you notice your eyes, nose and every single part of your face and would want to care about it. When this happens, we work towards betterment, we try to give the best of ourselves, be it going to the gym to maintain our shape, following a skincare routine for skin or anything. I love myself beyond words and there exists no substitute for that. This year witnessed struggles against modern apartheid or judging people on the basis on their skin tone. I would like to voice out my vote for them, we are beautiful the way we are. Our identity is our pride be it white, black, caucasian or brown.

There exist few who confuse being beautiful to being fair. Fairness in terms of skin tone is due to genes and other external factors which most of us don't have control over. Beauty is never dependent on the colour of the skin. It depends on the personality, of course, the face structure and the efforts we make to keep our skin healthy. If being fair is beauty then Ms Tunzi, the Miss Universe 2019 would have never made it even into the initial rounds of the pageant competition. Beauty is dependent on elegance and definitely not on skin tone. Every tone is beautiful in its own way and has equal chances to be expressed and represented in society.

Then what really matters – HOW DO I LOOK BEAUTIFUL? We are always beautiful the way we are but to appear more beautiful the first and foremost things according to me would be – SMILE. There can never be a substitute for a sweet smile. It is the best greeting that one could offer apart from therapy to facial muscles. Smile is precious and remember to smile not just when you are happy, but when you intend to spread the joy. Smile is auto reciprocated, it is transferred from one to another effortlessly.

The next would be the body language of the person and the gestures they show towards others. Not many in this modern world are serious about their body language unless it is for the HR round or standing before the media. A common man encounters more displeasing gestures in his daily life than warm ones. They may not really be associated with us and might not affect us as a person but these are some basic qualities that must be imbibed into a person.

The final point I would stress on would be grooming to the occasion. I wouldn't advocate wearing a suit or wearing formal wear for all occasions but in the meantime not approve of coming in boxers and t-shirt to a restaurant. This might be because of the reason that I put up efforts when I go to meet someone, I undoubtedly exist in pyjamas inside my house, but I make sure to leave the doorstep properly groomed when I have to meet someone and in the same way, I expect others to appear presentable. I don't think it is too much to ask for. Getting to the main idea, my Instagram skincare blog. I wasn't the makeup person or someone who relies too much on skincare and stuff. Necessity is the mother of invention and the necessity I faced was my wedding, it was around the corner in a few months. I was all tanned in Singapore, thanks to the tropical heat. I had to somehow turn to my old self before engagement and that was my inspiration to turn towards skincare and makeup. I can't show up on my engagement as a studyaholic and so I began experimenting on products.

One can suggest me to visit salons and parlours but I needed a routine to follow and not a one-time service, I want to remain presentable for the rest of my life and in that case, one can't always rush to a parlour. So, I began resorting to youtube channels for advice and suggestion on skincare products and methodology. It was indeed a difficult process to find the right channel, the right blogger who gives legit information but it wasn't impossible. In a few weeks, I began experimenting on my skin and resulting were slowly visible. My next big step in getting into skincare was because of my US trip. I went to the US to visit my cousins and only then I knew the price difference. Skincare products were so damn cheap in the United States, it was then I knew the heavy-duty charges levied when they import beauty products from other countries.

This made me go haywire for skincare and I turned to a skincare product addict. Trust me the price difference was as huge as a product costing $7USD is priced around 3000INR. It is nearly 5-6 times the original price. Adding to my madness for skincare, the Black Friday sale was live in the country and I simply couldn't control myself from shopping, shopping and binge shopping. With makeup products, I also shopped for winter wear that I might be needing later in the year. I was sure that I was going to the UK, so I fulfilled my entire shopping desire with black Friday. It is really hard for women to settle with shopping but my US trip settled my shopping appetite for the time being.

Now that I had more than everything needed for my skincare, I began following it as regular as possible and I could see the results day after day. There are options like Ayurveda, Siddha and other alternative medicinal skin products but they never give the entire composition of the ingredients used, they require a longer incubation time, prone to cause allergies, so I decided to go to chemicals.

Knowledge is best shared and I decided to share my skincare experience to the world and that was when I decided to turn my private account to public. The response to that decision wasn't totally as expected. There were a lot of fake accounts who began following me and now that my account was open, it was hard to lay control over my followers. To keep fake accounts at the bay, I had to get into my followers list once a while, browse through every single account, judge them based on their activity and followers and then block if they don't seem legit. In the initial days, this was amongst my routine to keep my account safe from fake accounts. With increased content and followers, it was increasingly difficult to do the police job and at a point in time, I became so tired and realized this was nothing more than a mere waste of time and energy, so I chose to ignore.

Nothing happens exactly as we plan and that phenomenon is called life. So, this make-up venture wasn't the perfect one and there were a few bloopers and things did go wrong. I did learn from such screw-ups and improved myself in the time that came up. There were quite a few times such incidents happened and every single time, I tried iterating to not repeat it in the future.

The most common and basic mistake that a blogger makes is that he/she forgets to switch on the camera before they begin their tutorial or their reel and they miss the shot.

Unfortunately, the missed shot would be the best among a million trails before and after. Since I don't post much of videos and limit myself to pictures, I rarely have had that experience. One memorable incident happened at my wedding blues. It was my engagement in the morning followed by a cocktail party in the evening and we hosted it at Radisson blu, Coimbatore. I was the new make-up artist in the family and I wanted this event to be a platform to prove it amongst my cousins. So, I began helping others with their make-up and it was near time for the party when I realized that I wasn't ready.

I was so busy prepping up my younger sister so that she happens to be the best bridesmaid ever and lost track of time in it. For that short period in time, I turned more of a make-up artist than that of a bride and went on with make-up. Once it was time, they were all rushing and gushing me up, to get on the stage considering the belief people have for the auspicious time. Under pressure, I came upon the stage with a not so proper make-up or in other words rush makeup and things went on. Everything except for my make-up was perfect, now that I wasn't proper for my own engagement the next step, I had to do was to cover my track. I couldn't afford a leak of these pictures into social media. It was fine among my family; they have dealt me from childhood and this wasn't really going to have any impact on them.

I tried my best to hide it from Instagram and Facebook. I restricted myself from posting any pictures of that day and kept Aakash and a few of my friends from doing the same. It was a lesson that I learnt and made sure in my head to have my make-up done before rushing to help others. The next on the schedule was our wedding and I can't afford any screw-ups at that time. I had the facts written deep in my mind, it was a once in a lifetime event and I screw up this, it was going to remain a screwup and can't be undone. I was careful about my make-up and skincare routine. I was so aware and alarmed of the previous mistake that I decided to go for a mock make-up before the wedding. I know but this is exactly as it sounds; I did go for mock wedding make-up, days before my actual wedding to make sure I don't screwup this time.

Another important thing was once in lifetime events like this must get into my blog. To get into my blog it mustn't be demotivating. So, I did my practice and had all that I require handy beforehand. The trial make-up session was more like a simulation of the real session, so I was able to approximate the time and accessories that I would need for the day and kept it all ready. At the dawn of the wedding, I was my priority and my goal that morning was to get ready, get complete. I kept telling myself, I must help others only if I am ready. I was able to execute my makeup as planned and there were no screwups, the schedule was packed. Finally, I had the confidence to post it on social media as there weren't any screwups. It wasn't more of a mistake but one good thing that I learnt.

The most important part of managing a blog is not just selecting and posting content but handling the critics. Critics in the other countries might come up with genuine suggestions feedback to improve the blog but here in our country most of the criticism is completely aggressive bullshit. There are very few who give genuine suggestions and feedback on my posts and the greater part of the criticism is crap. It is filled with so much negativity and abuse that it actually scared me in the beginning but sadly such people co-exist in every society and we have to deal with them.

Before conceiving this skincare blog, all I cared was to produce good genuine content for my followers and to give suggestions that would help them improve their skin but only after I turned my account public, I knew the negativity and the hatred people have. Though this hatred is unisexual, the greater portion affected is women.

In our country, when a woman starts a blog or tries to do something new, the first opposition for her venture comes from her family, in my case, they were always super supportive and the next line of opposition would be from the society, fortunately, social media lacks the feature of sharing rumours, easing the pressure. The next would be from the jobless stalkers and unfortunately, a lot of such people seem to exist in social media and they are more or less always active. The simple sign up procedure designed by social networks is taken as their advantage to create multiple fake accounts and threaten and disturb people's peace of mind online.

It is simply astonishing to look at the extent such threats could get from general verbal abuse to sending inappropriate content. At first, there were a few hate messages followed by criticism stating that I wasn't a dermatologist to address for skin care needs and I made it very clear to them that I never claimed to be a dermatologist or anything of that sort. This was something that could be taken and explainable.

The worst part of having the blog was comments from random fake accounts and disturbing messages. It was one or two in the initial phase but as my followers increased so did the number of spammers. Abusive comments and messages were describing me and assaulting me. When the entire blog is about skincare and makeup, I don't understand the need to verbally assault me or describe me.

When the blog isn't about me or my body, then I really don't understand the reason behind people body-shaming me.

It isn't cool to text or threaten someone or abuse them online. Spreading hate messages is against the community guidelines of social media and still, these people fail to understand that. Instead of using an anonymous or a fake account, they could very much use their own account, if they really wanted to tell something. When there exist fear in them and their conscience can't clear it right, then why must they do it? Provided it's a total waste of time. The possible response that I could offer was to ignore such messages and move on with my life. The most common reaction to an abusive message would be to ignore it, then get to that account – report and block it.

The hard part is that there are a lot of coward humans on social media or maybe a few who take the strain to create multiple accounts right after I block one and spread the hate. One threat among the many I received was that one despo or a retard spotted me in Coimbatore and threatened to kidnap me. It was threatening and scary but I at least believe that India hasn't gone that bad when it comes to women safety. When there are countries that decide the verdict for rapists on spot and execute it immediately, our country does it through a series of hearings, judge the girl, then the boy and only after that, the verdict is announced. This verdict would be soon challenged by the human rights activist and in some 5-10 years the accused would be punished. We often tend to forget that justice delayed is more or less justice denied.

The next level of harassment to a blogger, if she can handle verbal or threats via texts would be pictures. A few don't feel any shame in sharing disgusting pictures of their genitals to a woman online. Well about that – women never get fascinated or turned on looking at such pictures and if you expect them to develop some feelings on you by seeing your genitals then pardon me you are absolutely wrong. These people have no damn fucking idea on the irritation and disgust such pictures bring to women.

It simply isn't right to send inappropriate pictures just because you can send anything on Instagram. I did have starting trouble handing these but soon I decided to take it public by posting screenshots of those who do it on my story. The worst part that I never anticipated was a few people needed such publicity and were taunting me to post their chats on my story and sent me inappropriate pictures. I was glad to do it and soon I realized that this wasn't moving to an end. The more the accounts I report and block, the greater were the accounts that came, it simply turned to a never-ending vicious cycle. The only end to this was to take it to their own friends and followers. So I took all the time and strain to send the message screenshots of such proud men to their followers on Instagram. This made them get to their senses in an instant and made them address me as a sister, while they initially didn't mind addressing me as a slut. That was my solution after a few trails to stop such people.

As you might expect the threat wasn't just for me but to my boyfriend too, they threatened him about the things they would do to me and him if they had us but that was among our least worries and these are now the most common issues faced by influencers and bloggers. Be it profession, passion or any work we do, we would have our critics but the extent such people could get must be noted. A few psychopaths could get more serious as they may not just deliver their hate via text or by sharing pictures but could get obsessed and might even try to attack in real life and at such times the best and the most suitable option would be to raise a complaint or file an FIR.

There have been mixed comments regarding posting screenshots on my stories, but when such offenders don't take any shame in sharing such pictures, why should I? I also justify by stating when these perverts are bold enough to threaten someone mature like me, then the stake of women who can't handle situations would be horrible and it poses a greater threat on them, so I took it public on behalf of those who have been silent to such online harassment.

We live in a country with so much freedom and minimal security irrespective of gender. There exist violations at every single place and a few are simply tired and exhausted of such violations that they are used to it. There are a lot of instances were pictures and videos of women are morphed by few and released into the internet. We must understand that such online harassment isn't going to help and the culprits in this aren't just the ones who morph images but also those who like and share such pictures. The blame is shed equally on everyone's shoulder. I have heard from a few people about the stereotyping and judgement that our society has when someone whistle-blows such incidents but in the same time, I have also received some compliments from a few for being brave and facing things instead of losing hope.

There are a lot of women who are put into trauma, stress and fear because of such online threats and improper messages, sadly a few have even lost their lives because of this. The one possible excuse accusers advocate is they did it was for fun and never intended it to get so serious but isn't it too serious for fun and horrible to note how cruel and retarded their intentions could get for the sake of foolish pleasure. A few might do it for their physical pleasure which lasts for a few seconds or minutes but the victim is being affected psychologically for a time period much longer than their pleasure and that is something that needs serious care. Such retards must be psychologically addressed if it isn't possible to morally treat them.

CHAPTER V

Wo(ah̤)men

India is a country were rivers are named after women, women are worshipped as goddesses in temples and assaulted in their own homes or the roads of their city. The nation is portrayed as a woman known as the "Bharatmaata" while in the streets many women are getting raped and in the houses where photos and idols of Durga, Lakshmi, Saraswati are kept domestic abuse of all sort is staged and the entire country is a mute witness to it. 88 rape cases are recorded in this country almost every single day and close to 900 cases are filed under the category – crimes against women. These numbers are just the ones reported and out large there are thousands of unreported violent acts happening against women. Around 35% of women in the country have been victims of domestic violence physically and the scarier part is that 60% of the previous number is because of their partner.

Throwing some light on to the role of women in this lockdown, when the entire family remained in the house for around 3 months, there has been an alarming rise in the rate of violence reported against women. Domestic abuse has reached the highest in this quarantine, to be more specific marital rape occurrence have increased by 30% than normal. One major reason for this is stress and depression due to lack of job opportunities. Most if not all, of domestic violence, happens in families that fall below the poverty line and their economic weakness is one prime reason for such incidents to happen. Most of the people in this section, have to work every single day to earn their bread and factors of job security, insurance don't even come into play.

When such people are unemployed and have no other means to earn, they enter a zone of depression. Prolonged depression turns to an undirected rage and to quench the rage in their minds they tend to resort it either physically or verbally on someone. The only possible resort that such men could get is women at home, who aren't physically as strong. This rage is one of the most common reasons for domestic violence.

The second major reason for such domestic violence in the lockdown period is because of the withdrawal syndrome. When addiction is abruptly stopped without proper guidance or medical support they tend to behave inhumane and experience symptoms like lack of appetite, convulsions, dizziness etc... The unprecedented lockdown situation forced the closure of all liquor shops in the state pushing liquor addicts to this syndrome. As they are forced out of something that was once their everyday habit, the anger has made them resort to violence. The women in the house are the only anger therapy known to these men.

The more horrible fact is that not just adult women are being abused, but even children are being beaten, tortured and in the worst-case raped. When it becomes difficult for such psychologically retarded men to take it to women in the house like wife or sister, they tend to show it on children. The so-far average age for such abuses against children is 3 years. A child is abused when she hasn't fully learnt to talk and walk and that is amongst the biggest shame that the nation has to face. We all share posts about the perks of being a child and we share our opinion stating we didn't want to grow but what would be the mindset of such children who are being abused and treated no more than an object.

The more grieving part is that 60 per cent of crime against children including rape and assault are carried out by someone who is known to the children and not through a stranger which puts the safety of children on the brink. When children aren't safe enough in their own house, amongst their relatives, then where else could they grow up safe? I was shocked to see news stating "A man raped his own daughter" and I was more offended at the news channel on calling him a man instead of an animal. Such crimes have sadly increased in this lockdown and more women and children are being harassed in their own homes.

The positive part of lockdown is that women have turned out to be more independent. They have chosen to follow their passion, convert hobbies into a profession and a few have even made money out of it. This lockdown has provided women ample time to think, work and establish their passion and hobbies be it painting, cooking or embroidery. A lot of women have discovered their strong points and have begun working on them.

We all would have seen the rise in Instagram blogs and businesses in this lockdown, a lot of women have decided to use their skills to make money at least to fend for their micro expenses if not for everything. We have this custom, where the role of a man in this society would be to earn money and meet expenses of the family while the role of an ideal woman in the family would be to take care of the house chores and cook for the family. In accordance with this belief, most of the women don't find it necessary to put the effort to make money though they have the skills for it. That was something that changed in this lockdown and women are interested to experiment on their skills and to show it out to the world.

I have heard from a few followers that "they have discovered a new skill in this lockdown (like baking, painting) and are willing to invest the profit made from this skill to care for their skin". Another similar message stated her financial dependency on her parents and her happiness of being stable financially because of her blog. This may not account to huge turnover or 6-digit figures but these small figures would mean a lot more than just money and would help them choose their expenses and at least make them independent for one expense and that is one less requisition and that is a big feat in our country.

Different pages have come up for baking, crochets, painting, clothes, embroidery and a lot more. Apart from the benefit that it does to the women who manage and invest time in it, it has created a small micro market environment on Instagram. Monopoly bakeries or companies that produce such products now have to revise their prices and are forced to cut down their profits for their survival and Instagram as a marketplace is simple, cost-effective and efficient.

This is the real women empowerment that many leaders, reformers talked about. Empowerment like this mustn't be boosted by lockdown or quarantine but must come out of self-driven passion and interest, if not via motivation from others. There exists an ancient belief stereotyping woman are those who get married to someone else in due course of time and investing in their education is considered to be a waste of time. This stereotype is slowly changing in society and we could witness a lot of new talents and startups emerging from women.

In the life of a common Indian woman, there never is the deletion of a role, it is always been addition and as time passes the burden only adds and multiplies but never subtracts or get divided till she dies. This quarantine is no exemption to the roles and duties bestowed on her. Though in TV, news and social media, popular celebrities are seen helping women playing roles in cooking, cleaning and washing, the life of people in the country is far different from those of celebrities.

In the early days of her life, she plays the role of a daughter where she is forced to compromise her wishes and dreams for the sake of society and to keep up the ideal girl stereotype. Every dream that she tries to pursue is kept by asking her to "try it after marriage". The biggest threat to an outlying woman is that no-one would marry a non-ideal woman. Fortunately, that is changing slowly. Once married, there are a lot more roles added to her such as that of a wife, of a daughter-in-law, a sister-in-law and a lot more, in addition to the existing roles. She has to put up with her newly found family and make love to her man. She turns pregnant somewhere in between these two nd that would be the end of her personal life after which she has to care for the child, grow the child and a loop begins with roles being added. In the final days of her life, she is supposed to take care of her grandchildren, update to their level in the best case and on the worst case, her children ditch her at an old age home where she spends the life before death and passes away.

This is the general schedule of life of most of the women in our country and there certainly are a few exemptions to this cycle but only a few. Such exemptions are often shamed by society and clamped down to make sure that it doesn't turn to a trend. In this quarantine, men did clean their house, wash the dishes, help in cooking but the reason behind this wasn't really to help their partners or women in the house. If they really wanted to help their wives and mothers, then they wouldn't need this quarantine to help the women in the house and would have begun doing it long back.

It is sad to realise that the role of women is taken to be a hobby, game or entertainment for men. In fact, many were bored out of their minds in this lockdown which led them to take up such roles. The worst part is that they consider it cool to take videos or pictures of them working at home and share it among their friends and colleagues. They fail to understand that the women in the house also have a life beyond vessels and clothes in the house. It isn't very pleasing for them, most of the time to manage the house, most of the women might have had different dreams and ventures to pursue before their marriage and those three knots have trapped them at home forever.

Men if not possible to share the responsibility must at least try to give their best to understand the importance of women in their everyday lives. They must try and play their role in maintaining the house as it isn't only the curse of the women in the house but everyone residing in the house. It mustn't be taken as something inferior, as no work is ever inferior to another.

India is amongst the very few countries in the world where women are highly stereotyped. When the law guarantees fundamental freedom and guarantees a woman of all rights that men could enjoy, the bigger law in the action is the society. The most retarded, superstitious old men and women of the country form this society and use it to keep the country from progressing, not just from this point of view but generally when there is some good thing about to happen, some change about to take form, they shut it out by claiming the alignment of the planets, by astrology and their damn knowledge.

Our Vedas though written 4000-5000 years old have the message required for the modern generation and there is no doubt about it. Our tradition provides a solution to almost every problem that might ever happen to mankind. For instance, the yoga formulated my sadhus and yogis are effective enough for us in the 21st century in the field of health and well-being. If our Veda's and scriptures are this accurate then where does the glitch happen? Why our women consider inferior to men? Why are they stereotyped?

The biggest problem lies in the communication from one generation to another, most of the traditional and cultural beliefs were transferred orally and plenty of Vedic manuscripts were destroyed by invaders and conquerors. The oral knowledge that is passed down has seen changes based on the level of understanding people possess. Looking into a simple habit of trimming our nails, there is a belief that nails mustn't be trimmed after sunset. The fact behind it was that days before electricity was invented, there was very less light available after sunset and trimming at that time might cause accidental injury to our fingers. But the communication gap has linked trimming of nails with days and astrology. A few people state not to cut nails on Tuesday and Friday and claim it to bring bad luck to the family.

The boundaries laid to women might have come from similar gaps as even the gods that we worship preach men and women as equals. Such communication gaps must have happened around the 17th century where atmost confusion and chaos happened in the Indian subcontinent due to invasions and wars. A few retards must have modified these beliefs at that time for their benefits. The first and most awful stereotypes, I have ever witnessed comes from the commercial advertisements for sanitary napkins. This is where it all begins, in almost all the advertisements and commercials for sanitary napkins like the whisper, the blood that is supposed to flow as a result of menstruation is shown in blue colour and not the true red colour. This is the most common social stigma against menstruation when a product designed to target women at times of menstruation itself stigmatizes blood which is a component of every single human and decides to telecast it as a blue liquid instead of red, then how could we normalize things related to women?

This is the 21st century and we have known a lot about the highest point of earth, the deepest point in our ocean and everywhere in between including our physiology. It is the nature of human females to menstruate as a part of their reproductive cycle and being the most evolved species till date, it is so far the most sophisticated adaption to help ensure survival. Students from grade 8 are being taught about reproduction, menstruation and other factors in their school curriculum to understand the nature and respect the differences. They are trained as per curriculum to take it as science and evolution but that always remains just for marks, as they step out, they take the mythical judgmental side.

Menstruation is considered the biggest taboo ever; people are not even supposed to talk about it in public. It is a crime if women during THOSE days worship god and in a few areas, they are even forbidden to sleep on the bed. They are considered sinners and treated as untouchables. The worst part is that retail and medical shops that sell sanitary napkins pack them discretely either in a black cover or wrap it in a newspaper and give it to their customers. When every woman in this world goes through this phenomenon and almost every man who has ever had a sister, wife or mother would know about it, then for whose sake is this kept a secret? Why are they packed discretely?

These questions can never be answered because it is US, we know the science, we might be educated but we still choose to follow such practices and stigmatise women. Our intention may not be to hurt them or make them feel awkward but our parents followed it, so we follow it. Our parents followed it because their parents did, maybe tracing back to a few generations, they might have not known the facts about it, there might have been some issues regarding this and hence they might have followed it. One possible explanation is that there exists a chance of spread of germs when menstrual blood falls somewhere public, blood stains are permanent hence people restrained from sleeping on the bed but that must be times when the sanitary pads weren't invented and women had to rush to the restrooms to discharge their flow. The modern generation has to a certain improved and crossed most of those limitations and hence we must adapt ourselves to the new improvements and modify our practices.

The next most stereotyped topic is about sex, women aren't allowed to talk about their sexual interests in public. One could find hundreds of posts in the social media or memes about masturbation or self-pleasure but it refers an act performed by men, it is either described as hilana or shaking the anaconda but we fail to understand the fact that women are also entitled to such pleasure and they do have the right to talk or discuss it. When it is common for a man to beat his meat or jest about porn or masturbation, then it must also be common among women to talk the same but it isn't. There is a lot of stereotyping, stigmatism and discrimination when it comes to women.

I don't understand the broad difference, except for the physiology. The feelings, hormones and the drive are more similar and common for both genders, then why don't people normalize the topic, ease the pressure on these things?

Even after marriage, females have very less freedom to talk to their partners about sex, their interests in sex. We live in a country where two strangers meet up to make a bond called marriage, but still, it ought to be discussed. Women are forced to treat husband as their masters and it is more of a lady's duty to give in to his wishes. She is not allowed to express her opinions, talk about her likes or dislikes but has to go with anything that her husband does.

When men could have their pleasure zones like the position and place then women must also be entitled to express and demand her comfort in the intercourse. It isn't something that must be granted or requested but is more of a right that she earns. The most important or the most essential part of a relationship must be mutual consent and most of the women in Indian households don't even have that word in their dictionaries. They consider it a duty like cooking and more often are being devoured like animals. They are at times even abused, bruised but they aren't supposed to talk about it outside, because it is considered as a crime to express it out.

The next myth is about the difference in the physique of a man and a woman. These are differences that are necessary for the continuity of life and not a question of character or deeds. We don't stigmatise a shirtless man while we don't hesitate to call a woman in the same state – a bitch. We stigmatise for their structure but we also have to agree to the fact that without this structure, it is nearly impossible for any mammal to reproduce or grow a healthy child, only women can bear and grow a child. That is the power of women and we treat her inferior.

If the above reasons aren't yet convincing that women are being treated inferior, then what do you think is the first response for a rape case?

If we think straight, it would be to seek medical care for the woman, nab the offenders and punish them. But the procedure followed here is slightly different. If the incident happens somewhere rural, the best possible solution there would be to marry the girl to the same guy who raped her, they consider it as defending her honour but that would just give him the advantage to do anything to that girl. The second custom is to question the character of the girl and judge her.

If the same happens in a city, the girl will first be judged by her own parents who instead of supporting the girl might consider her a disgrace to the family and try to cover things up. They would want the girl to remain mute and then lay control on her freedom like not to go out late in the night, don't wear shorts, skirt above knees etc.

If the parents are supportive enough to take it to the court, then there it would be made public and every media would cover this sensationally not to ensure justice for the girl but to make sure their TRP peaks. The first question the cops raise wouldn't be about the accusers but about the girl, her dressing, they would enquire about the girl's affairs, character and societal notions and then get on with the case. They then would begin the investigation and try to find the culprit, even if they find the culprit, hand them before the law and it would take years in trails, enquiry and by the time the verdict is announced, the punishment is served, the victim would have lost all hope on justice and the other hand would be the debate topic of the entire nation.

Our country and the society would blame the victim, her parents for the rape and do you still think we don't treat our women inferior?

CHAPTER VI

Bundles to betterment

This quarantine woke the skincare enthusiast and drove me to make my blog and address people's concern on skincare. Talking about, or reviewing and recommending a product on social media isn't the skincare solution. A few found it difficult to shop for the exact product as copies exist in the market, while others found it difficult to locate the product because most of it wasn't available in the local stores or the pharmacies.

When such issues surfaced up on my account, I realized that I can't just share reviews on products that weren't in the reach of my followers. I somehow must make it available to my followers and the solution for that need was "The Bundles". I first proposed this idea amongst my friends and they were more excited than I was, so why not give it a try. The initial orders of the bundle were prepared without tagging a price on my service. But

IF YOU ARE GOOD AT SOMETHING, NEVER DO IT FOR FREE!

I was investing a lot of time in this and to keep it going, I can't do it with a price so I quoted a small price for my service. My friends were instrumental in spreading the word, about my new hobby turned business and put-up stories and statuses on their social handles, that was not all but a few of them turned to my most regular customers too.

I would technically quote I was helping to find the right product for the Indian skin and very few people do that, anyone could suggest, recommend products for the skin but I keep it specific concentrating on Indian people and that would be my unique selling point. If you think this is easy money business, trust me it isn't.

It is time-taking, I make it a point to go through every single ingredient and research about it deeply before choosing it. You never know about the specific side effects; a product could have and the adversity it could cause on the skin. I never would want that to happen to any of the customers who trust me and hence the time. It takes 3-5 hours per order for the selection and I don't go for it unless I am sure.

The major problem that I encountered in this small venture of mine was there were a few who defaulted on the payment. I was more of fed-up of this behaviour and that was when I began switching from postpaid to prepaid.

The largest support for my service came from my family, they were really helpful. Most of my customers were friends of my relatives and family friends, that was how the entire referral system worked. Quality and satisfaction are something that many people are desperate for, when you give authentic and quality products then they come back to you for more, not many firms in the modern-day offer quality as they compromise on quality for the prices, but there do exist people who consider quality over price.

After using my products, the initial customers that I had were more than satisfied and they came back along with their friends to order more and I was happy to help. Not everyone was happy with this and there were a few who were trying to copy me without any innovation, they were exactly doing everything that I did but with very less knowledge and information. Competition is always appreciated but such cut-throat competition is more of a cheap trick to earn money but weren't able to cater to the exact needs and eventually ran out of business.

The bundles soon turned to a family of 150 happy customers. They trusted me for their skin and ordered from me by default. I moved to the UK for my masters and the bundles' program had to pause, but family is always family and I can't turn them down. Hence, I still don't turn down an order and help my customers select the best for their skin.

www.ingramcontent.com/pod-product-compliance
Lightning Source LLC
LaVergne TN
LVHW042003060526
838200LV00041B/1844